WIRE WRAP JE\
MAKING

The Essential Beginner's guide to learn the tools, patterns and techniques to make amazing wire wrapped projects like bracelets, pendants, rings and beads like a pro

Chloe Ethan

copyright@2021

Table of contents

CHAPTER ONE

INTRODUCTION TO WIRE WRAP JEWELRY

Wire wrap jewelry technique has grown to become very popular over the years. It has gone ahead to make way for an entire exhibition of awesome jewelry designs without the need for a huge number of tools.

This jewelry method can fuse anything in the process. It all depends on what you want. From gemstone cabochons, to charms, to gemstone beads, beads etc. it's a complete pure wire work.

In the accompanying pages, I will be giving the tips, guidance and procedures in different areas of wire wrapping and are available to open to all levels of jewelry makers.

Wire wrapping is a skill that anyone can learn with determination and become a pro in making jewelries. The beautiful thing about creating wire wrapped gems or jewelries is that there is no particular method of going about it – you can make free shape designs with your wire, so making wire wrapped earrings is a fantastic path for tenderfoots to begin.

Wire wrapping can be utilized to produce a loop for combining various parts, for example, while making a wrapped wire circle or wrapping a pendant. Through wire wrapping, you can likewise tie down beads to a structure, or even connect non bead things, for example, wire wrapping rhinestone cup chain onto a bangle. At the point when wrapped, bended, bowed and controlled, the wire itself can turn into the structure and establishment of your piece or go about as a design detail. Wire wrapping lets you make custom shapes and edges, and gives you more approaches to utilize various parts together.

Wire wrapping is a skill that anyone can learn with determination and become a pro in making jewelries. The beautiful thing about creating wire wrapped gems or jewelries is that there is no particular method of going about it – you can make free shape designs with your wire, so making wire wrapped earrings is a fantastic path for novices to begin.

Recommended Tools for
WIRE WRAPPING

Round nose pincers - for molding and bowing wire

Side cutters - for cutting wire

Kill nose pincers (otherwise called chain nose forceps) - incredible generally useful pincers, useful for molding and getting to hard to arrive at places

Level nose forceps - assists with making sharp corners in the wire

Then again, we additionally offer a total bunch of forceps and side cutters which incorporate the entirety of the above just as bent nose pincers (helpful for difficult to arrive at places) all these comes in one handy case.

CHAPTER TWO

HOW TO WIRE WRAP A BEAD

Wire wrapping a bead is a
straightforward wire wrapping
strategy however simply needs

a little determination to create smart and steady outcomes.

When you have mastered the process, you will have the ability to make a wide scope of excellent gemstone jewelry.

The accompanying bit by bit guidelines tell the best way to make this method which is especially fit to utilizing with gemstone beads that have little openings. This is on the grounds that the 0.3mm (28 check) wire is extremely fine and adaptable and is extraordinary for wire wrapping.

Be that as it may, you can make similar impact with bigger holed beads and wires that are thick, it will simply be a smaller more troublesome! We suggest beginning little so you can dominate the procedure effortlessly.

Tools Required

- Side cutters

- Round nose forceps

- Snipe nose forceps

Materials Needed

- Metal wire - 0.3mm, check the wire will fit through your picked bead

- Gemstone bead

Adhere To Our Step By Step Instructions on How to Wire Wrap a Bead

Stage 1

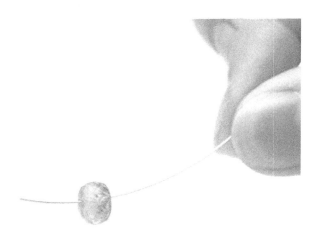

Cut a length of wire roughly 10cm long (it is simpler to have some additional wire than you will really use, as it gives you more to clutch while wrapping). Slip your dot onto the wire, leaving roughly 2cm toward one side (the opposite end will be longer).

Stage 2

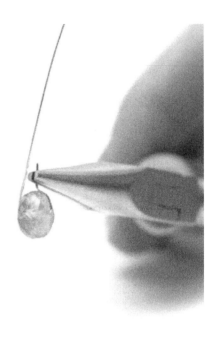

Squeeze or pinch the two finishes of the wire together at the highest point of the bead. Watch that the bead is focused.

Stage 3

Remove the finish of the short side of the wire utilizing side cutters, so it is just around 2-3mm over the bead.

Stage 4

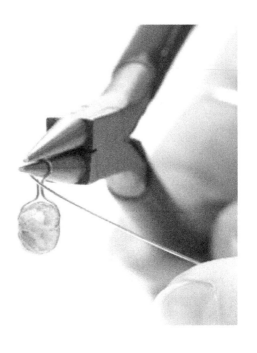

Next create a circle or loop with the more extended side of wire by bowing it to a correct point and folding it over the tip of your round nose pincers. Ensure the circle is over the finish of the

short side of the wire and
middle of the bead.

Stage 5

Utilizing snipe nose forceps, hold
the circle level between the tips.
Take hold on the long length of

the wire and hold it between your fingers and ensure you keep it tight. Begin folding it over the stem of the wires - beginning at the base of the circle and working down towards the bead. Ensure that each wrap sits perfectly and near the previous one.

Stage 6

At the point when you arrive at the highest point of the bead trim the end conveniently with side cutters. On the off chance that there is a sharp end left, twist it delicately with the kill nose pincers so it sits level and is tucked neatly away.

Wrapped up!

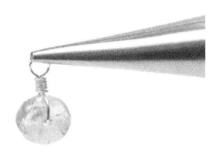

Your wrapped bead is presently
completed and prepared to join
into a wonderful adornments or
jewelry design. Recall that this
method takes practice (and a
little persistence) to dominate.

So continue on in the event that it doesn't look as you needed on your first endeavor or examination with the strategy until you discover a way that works for you.

Whenever you have dominated this strategy you will think that it's helpful for some, extraordinary beading projects. Wire wrapped beads like this can be joined with a hop ring to a part of chain and made into drop studs and pendants or connected to a wristband to make charms - the prospects are perpetual!

CHAPTER THREE

HOW TO CREATE A WIRE WRAPPED GEMSTONE RING

Wire wrapping is so well known and it's no big surprise with all the stunning and special designs you can make!

In this bit by bit instructional exercise, I tell you precisely the best way to make a wire wrapped ring utilizing a rough gemstone. Above we've utilized a similar procedure with a piece of ocean glass and harsh amethyst stone.

Wire-wrapping doesn't need any binding supplies, and with a couple of apparatuses required you can make a straightforward ring in a few minutes.

TIP: It's extraordinary to rehearse with plated silver wire

as a spending alternative however know it's harder to work with than real silver which is considerably more malleable.

REQUIREMENTS NEEDED

40cm of 0.8mm authentic silver round wire

A rough gemstone you desire

Side cutters

Triblet

Level nose forceps

Snip nose forceps

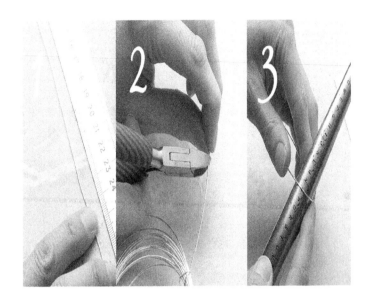

1. Lay the wire straight on a level surface and measure roughly 40cm.

2. Cut with side cutters - 40cm gives enough wire for your ring size and surplus wire for wrapping.

3. Start by tenderly twisting the wire into equal parts around the triblet.

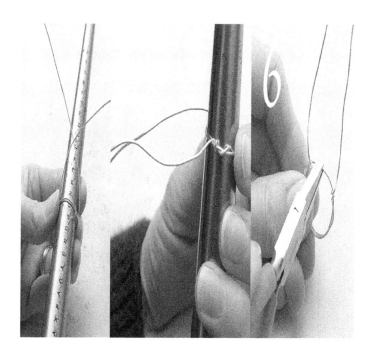

4. Place your wire work on the triblet on the position of the ring size that you'd preferred your

ring to be. In the event that you don't have a ring triblet you can check out the house for something round to utilize, for example, a wooden spoon handle, pen or wooden dowels. Fold one finish of the wire over the triblet, leaving two loose ends.

5. With the two remaining loose ends at the front of the triblet, independently wrap each end under the wire ring a couple of wraps, leaving enough space for the length of your stone between them. These wraps on either side will tie down the ring to a fixed size.

6. Position your level nose pincers where your stone will rest and utilize them to smooth the bend of the ring somewhat. This will give your stone a compliment surface to sit on, making it simpler to secure.

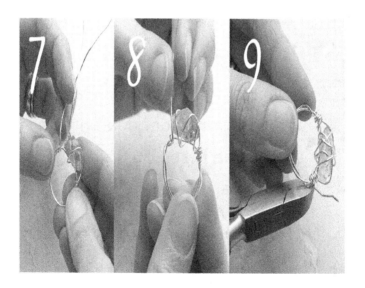

7. Hold the stone set up on the ring and fold one finish of the free wire over the stone to hold it set up. At the point when you run out of wire, fold additional circles over the side circles you made in sync 5 to make sure about set up.

8. Rehash stage 8 with the other piece of free wire and wrap at the contrary side, guaranteeing the stone is secure inside the wire wrap.

9. Utilize side cutters to clip off any free wire and use kill nose pincers to wrap up any loose ends that may exist. Position

your ring back on to the triblet
and re-shape to the right size.

Your ring is currently wrapped
up! Presently you know the
method, you can try by making
more loops and getting
inventive with your wire
wrapping!

CHAPTER FOUR

HOW TO MAKE A WIRE WRAPPED BEAD CHAIN

Transform YOUR Favorite GEMSTONE BEADS INTO A BEAUTIFUL CHAIN!

This page gives bit by bit guidelines on the most proficient method to wire wrap singular beads to shape a fragile beaded chain. Extraordinary for fusing in your necklace, wristband and earring designs.

This is an extraordinary technique to figure out how to facilitate many design options, it likewise causes your beads to go further.

In this instructional exercise we've utilized some amazonite beads that are roughly 8x5mm. As the opening in the bead is around 0.7mm, we decided to utilize 0.5mm real silver wire. You can utilize any beads of your choice and appropriate sized wire. You can utilize generally similar beads or make your own design with various shapes and distinctive colored gemstone beads.

MATERIALS NEEDED

Metal Wire

You can select from our collection of metal wire which include; plated, sterling silver, copper, 9ct gold, brass and lots more.

Pick an appropriate measurement wire for your beads, that will run easily through the openings (smaller beads = smaller openings). We would for the most part suggest utilizing somewhere in the range of 0.3mm and 0.5mm wire contingent upon your selection of beads.

Gemstone Beads

You will require a gemstone beads! We have such countless wonderful beads to select from. Gem stones come in the range of different sizes and shapes.

In this instructional exercise, we've utilized some amazonite beads like these.

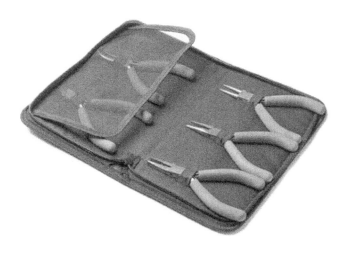

Pliers for Making Jewelry

This instructional exercise requires a couple of forceps to finish the look including round nose pincers, snipe nose pincers and side cutters. These are accessible separately or in our well known pack of forceps or pliers.

Carefully follow our wire wrapped bead chain tutorial below;

Stage 1

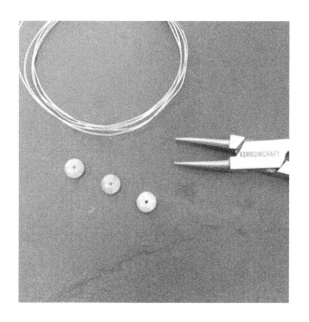

Line up your beads in your preferred order in which you want them to appear on the chain, this gives you a perfect of idea of how the finished work will look like.

Stage 2

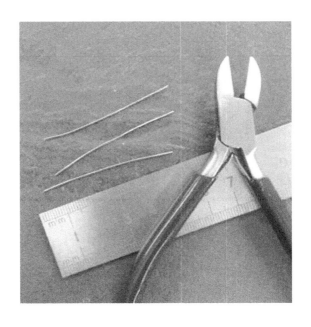

Utilize side cutters to cut a length of wire. Roughly 5cm of wire per bead ought to be enough, however remember diverse wire checks and bead sizes will require various lengths so it merits attempting a couple of first to see which will leave you with least wastage (the beads utilized here are around 5mm wide).

Tip: Having somewhat more wire than you need will make wrapping simpler.

Stage 3

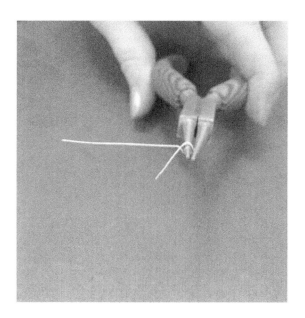

Take the main piece of wire and structure a circle one end utilizing the round nose forceps, leaving a short length one side of the loop.

Stage 4

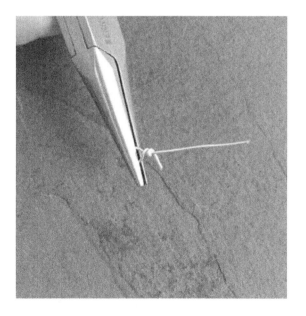

Take the shorter length of wire and fold it over the more drawn out length to make a tight perfect loop, 2 or 3 turns ought to be sufficient. You can utilize snipe nose pincers to help hold the wire whist wrapping.

Stage 5

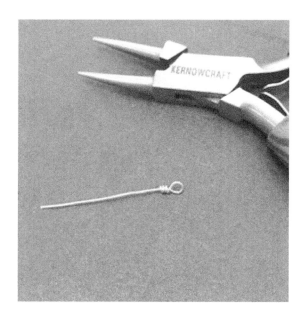

Utilize side cutters to remove any surplus wire as near the

loop as conceivable at that point utilize the snipe nose pincers to ensure it's wrapped up and there are no sharp points left. You should now have what resembles an eye pin with a circle toward one side that has been wrapped closed.

Stage 6

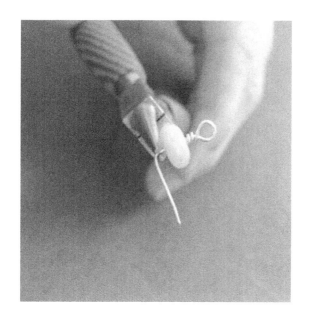

Thread the principal or first bead onto the open finish of the wire at that point place your round nose forceps after the bead and twist the wire to a correct angle.

Stage 7

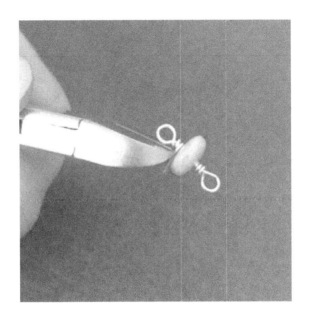

Structure another loop and replicate the interaction of firmly wrapping the wire down the pin towards the bead. Once more, remove any surplus wire as near the loop as conceivable at that point utilize the snipe nose pincers to ensure it's wrapped up and there are no sharp points left.

Stage 8

This should leave you with two circles either side of the bead and wire curls between the circle and the bead, the bead is currently secure on the wire.

Stage 9

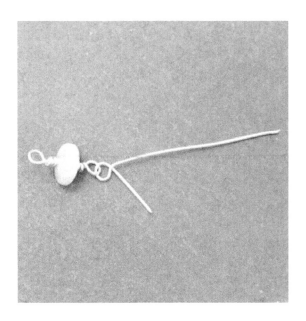

Presently you need to utilize this wrapping method to shape your chain. Start again by utilizing one of the lengths of wire and making a loop one end as in the past - this time stringing or threading the end loop of the past bead onto the circle prior to wrapping it closed.

Stage 10

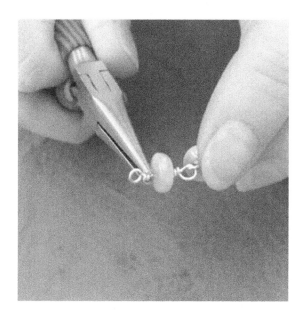

Keep on replicating these procedures until you arrive at your ideal length of chain.

Stage 11

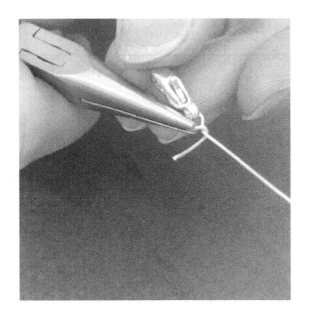

In the event that you need to add a fasten or clasp to your chain you can wrap it straight onto the chain similarly you appended a new link. On the other hand, you can utilize hop or split rings to join it.

Completed!

Your bead chain is currently
finished. You can make this look
with any completely drilled bead
of your choice!

CHAPTER FIVE

HOW TO CREATE A WIRE WRAPPED CABOCHON PENDANT

I have put together this instructional exercise on the best way to wire wrap a gemstone cabochon to make a lovely pendant. This venture utilizes one of our staggering spiderweb turquoise cabochons however you can utilize this method with any of your number one gemstones and decision of metal wire.

Follow carefully the step by step guide as listed here, and purchase all the gems making apparatuses and supplies you need online to get started.

Tools and Supplies Needed

- Flat nose pincers

- Round nose forceps

- Wire cutters

- 3x 20cm of 0.6mm wire (authentic silver wire in this task)

- 2x 15-20 cm of 0.3mm wire (authentic silver wire in this task)

- Approx 18x13mm cabochon or another appropriate size (included: spiderweb turquoise cabochon)

- Tape measure/ruler

- Necklet chain

- Optional: clamp

Carefully Follow My Step By Step Tutorial on Creating A Wire Wrapped Pendant Below

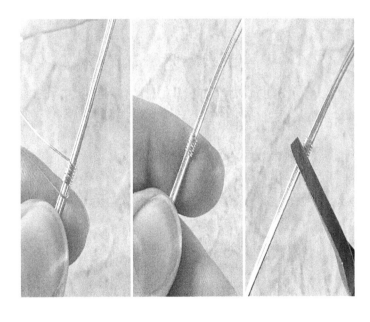

Take your 3 bits of 0.6mm 20cm base wires in a single hand, (in the event that you think that its simpler you can utilize a clamp to keep them straight), take 1 piece of the 0.3mm wire and in the wires, fold over the 3 base wires while holding them level around multiple times.

Cut the 0.3mm wire near the base wires with side cutters and utilize your level nose forceps to tenderly press together to make sure about.

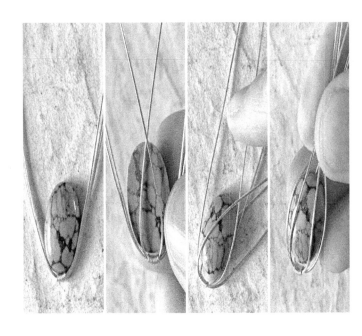

Position your cabochon down and with the joined wires at the base, tenderly curve the wires around the edges.

Turn your cabochon over in your grasp and tenderly draw the two back wires and get them over at the back, at that point turn the cabochon over and do likewise over the front of the stone.

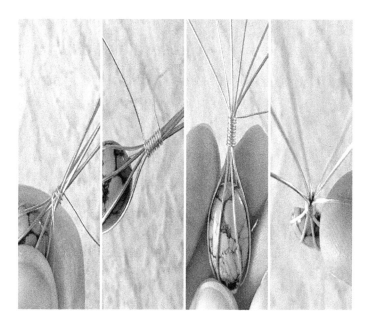

Bring all the wires around to the highest point of the cabochon and arrange.

Require your second piece of 0.3mm wire and wrap the wires together firmly, I did this around multiple times around, keeping the strain pleasant and educated to keep the cabochon set up and secure.

Trim off the wire with your side cutters and utilizing your level nose pincers, delicately press the end near the base wires.

Spread put your wires so two are looking ahead and two to one or the other side.

Delicately twist one wire aside and around the rear of the wrapped wires.

Fold over once ensuring the wire taught.

Utilizing your side cutters trim the wire, replicate this on the contrary side.

Whenever you have managed the two sides utilize your level nose forceps to make sure about the finishes against the base wires.

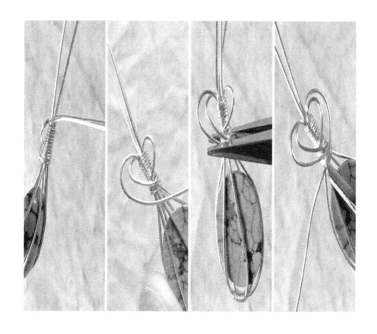

Go ahead and take the second wire along the edge of the 1st heart loop and fold over beneath the wires you have secured already.

Trim the wire with your side cutters and utilize level nose

pincers to tenderly press the wire to the base.

Replicate this process means on the opposite side.

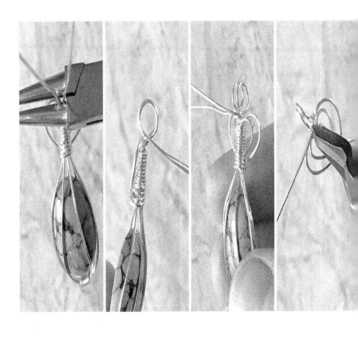

Take the last two wires and curve them advances to the front of the pendant.

Utilizing your round nose forceps, hold the wires as near the base as could reasonably be expected and twist them around the two wires on each side.

Take out the pincers and delicately twist around the front and to the back to ensure the loops are properly secured.

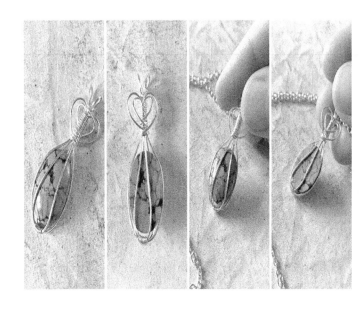

Your wire wrapped cabochon pendant is finished! Just add a string or chain to settle the piece prepared to wear.

Made in United States
North Haven, CT
26 December 2021

13600020R00039